urban haiku

Urban Haiku
Recent Work Press
Canberra, Australia

Copyright © Owen Bullock 2015

Standard Edition

National Library of Australia
Cataloguing-in-Publication entry.

Bullock, Owen

Urban haiku / Owen Bullock.

ISBN: 9780994456502 (paperback)

A821.3

All rights reserved. This book is copyright. Except for private study, research, criticism or reviews as permitted under the Copyright Act, no part of this book may be reproduced stored in a retrieval system, or transmitted in any form by any means without prior written permission. Enquiries should be addressed to the publisher.

Cover illustration: 'robotthing' © Lucy Bullock 2012
Cover design: Recent Work Press
Set in Saigon, 12 pt

recentworkpress.com

urban haiku

owen bullock

RECENT
WORK
PRESS

for Sue

heads sway
laughing at
the turbulence

Sydney airport
a huge Maori fella walks through
whistling *Greensleeves*

terminal
two men in green jackets
gesticulate wildly

.

the girl on the bus
combing
her mother's hair

a picture of a truck
beside the endless
highway

mall
I don't know what
the T-shirt means

Canberra's bird people
splashed liberally
with bird droppings

trees passing
in your sunglasses
on the dashboard

a line of cars follows the ambulance

before dawn
a leaf falls
from the sycamore

busy morning —
enjoying
the phone queue

seminar...
he slips *fascists*
into *fashion*

a student
with duct tape patches
on his knees

lakeside
the tease of wind
on water

a rainbow
draining off
the fountain

second storey balcony
a man polishes
a golf club

looks at his watch twice
as he crosses the road

tugging at my sleeve
a kite of spider threads
eucalypt leaves

moon's doggerel
a man at the bus stop
dressed like Phil Spector

lingering outside
before the bus leaves
smokers

an old car
in a paddock …
my sense of relief

a lost duckling
waddles
from one pond
to another

a feather floats
among the bubbles
this our world

eucalypt image
imposed on the water
without touch

looking long enough
invertebrates appear

the downy feather
smells of
duck belly

graffiti screams
at the impassive
wetlands

on the path
an old
pink bow

the half-eaten apple
half-rotted

8.56
waiting for the shop to open
to buy a cake tin

homeless man
picking up rubbish
on his patch

intersection a child drinks the rain

reading a war poem
she tears at
her hair

mid-afternoon
my student uses the word
'thusly'

painting of a philosopher
stares
till I can't disagree

in the pub misunderstanding Kant

driving in fog
the line beyond which
I can't see

butterfly shadow
becomes a leaf

a guy on the bus
reading a blue book
called *Anarchism*

museum
not enough
dust

sniffing the earth
I see
a cavernous mine

sick room
birds alight
in the leafless tree

full yellow moon
purple sky, my day
reaches its end

rush hour
a leaf swirls up
in the maelstrom

bus stop
one homeless man
introduces us
to another

bus window
the vein in a hand
on a hand-break

suburb
a two-humped camel
painted on a front door

air-hostess
head side to side
looking for rubbish

sunset flight
the wings
glow red

arrivals gate
kids in dressing gowns

talking about art
he foams
at the mouth

I don't care
which symphony it is
I just like it

in a margin of Proust
someone has made
a calculation

pulls out a shirt tail
to clean his glasses
leaves it untucked

home —
boarding pass
in recycling

man on a bicycle
a shirt on a hanger
hooked to his back

Anthropology —
she strides through the museum
rattling keys

after the event
his laughter
shakes the table

the guitarist
is a master
I relax into his hands

Friday afternoon
four boys playing touch
in the rain

pied stilt
its hesitant
bob

bus ride
her pigtail
hangs in my notes

old man's cardigan
such a comfortable
brown

arrivals gate
her face says
he's not here

grains of pollen
circle
in the lake

listening post
a hollow log
is my grave

tiles the Guides made
covering over with
water and soil

the little boy
at the bus stop says
flower is a bad word

blossom snow
Saturday night
lights up

walking to the festival
a woman with a laugh
like yours

I hear the Italian sing
and wish
I'd met you sooner

in the middle of their song
a car accelerates
in tune

old harmonica player
shaking his way
to life and death

the further
we walk together
the closer we are

Acknowledgements

Thanks to the editors and publishers of the following venues in which some of these haiku previously appeared:

Axon: Creative Explorations, *Chrysanthemum* (Austria), *Haiku in the Wetlands* (IPSI), *Kokako* (NZ), *paper wasp*, *Presence* (UK), *World Haiku Review*.

'sunset flight' and 'air-hostess' first appeared in the page-fold book *Redex* (Ampersand Duck, 2014).

'after the event', 'Anthropology' and 'a guy on the bus' first appeared in the chapbook *tracer* (Ampersand Duck, 2015).

Thanks to Shane Strange, Sue Peachey and Kathy Kituai.

Owen Bullock has published two previous collections of haiku, *wild camomile* (Post Pressed, Australia, 2009) and *breakfast with epiphanies* (Oceanbooks, NZ, 2012). His haiku have been published widely and anthologised. He has published a collection of poetry, *sometimes the sky isn't big enough* (Steele Roberts, NZ, 2010); the novella, *A Cornish Story* (Palores, UK, 2010), and a number of chapbooks of haiku and poetry, including *tracer* (Ampersand Duck, Canberra, 2015). He is a former editor of *Kokako*, New Zealand's only haiku magazine, and has edited numerous other journal issues and anthologies, most recently *Underneath — The University of Canberra's Vice-Chancellor's International Poetry Prize, 2015* (with Niloofar Fanaiyan). At the beginning of 2014 he moved to Australia to undertake a PhD in Creative Writing at the University of Canberra. He also juggles and plays the tin whistle.

www.ingramcontent.com/pod-product-compliance
Lightning Source LLC
Chambersburg PA
CBHW021135300426
44113CB00006B/440